STUDY GUIDE

RESTORE

90 DAYS OF INTENTIONAL LIVING

For foreign and subsidiary rights, contact the author.

Cover design by: Todd Petelle
Cover photo by: Andrew van Tilborgh

ISBN: 978-1-969062-23-0   1 2 3 4 5 6 7 8 9 10

Printed in the United States of America

STUDY GUIDE

RESTORE

90 DAYS OF INTENTIONAL LIVING

DANA GENTRY

FO
UR

CONTENTS

DAY 1.   **A FRESH START** 8

DAY 2.   **POWER OF MOMENTS** 10

DAY 3.   **WINNING: PART 1** 12

DAY 4.   **WINNING: PART 2** 14

DAY 5.   **PASSION** 16

DAY 6.   **PRESSURE** 18

DAY 7.   **INVESTMENT MINDSET** 20

DAY 8.   **TWO TYPES OF PEOPLE** 22

DAY 9.   **MISSING THE MARK** 24

DAY 10. **CONTENTMENT** 26

DAY 11. **PERSPECTIVE** 28

DAY 12. **THE FIVE Ps OF SUCCESS** 30

DAY 13. **THE FOUR Cs** 32

DAY 14. **THINKING HIGHER** 34

DAY 15. **YOUR UNIQUENESS** 36

DAY 16. **BEING A GIVER** 38

DAY 17. **SERVING** 40

DAY 18. **YOUR BEST DECADE EVER** 42

DAY 19. **THRIVE IN A DOWNTURN** 44

DAY 20. **THE BEST OF THE BEST** 46

DAY 21. **HAPPINESS** 48

DAY 22. **LEADERSHIP TOOLKIT** 50

DAY 23. **THE FIVE WELLS OF A MOREHOUSE MAN** 52

DAY 24. **A REVERENCE** 54

DAY 25. **WHY NOT YOU?** 56

DAY 26. **SEVEN INTENTIONAL LUNCH QUESTIONS** 58

DAY 27. **PERSONAL DEFINITION OF SUCCESS** 60

DAY 28. **WISDOM** 62

DAY 29. **JOY** 64

DAY 30. **OBEDIENCE** 66

DAY 31. **CHOICES** 68

DANA GENTRY

RESTORE
90 DAYS OF INTENTIONAL LIVING

IN
LIFE
FAITH
BUSINESS

DAY 32. **BE A COFFEE BEAN** 70

DAY 33. **INCREASING YOUR CAPACITY FOR STRESS** 72

DAY 34. **BECOMING THE YOU OF YOUR INDUSTRY** 74

DAY 35. **NEVER SPLIT THE DIFFERENCE:**
THE POWER OF NEGOTIATION 76

DAY 36. **BECOMING YOUR FUTURE SELF** 78

DAY 37. **THE SIX HUMAN NEEDS:**
UNDERSTANDING WHAT DRIVES YOU 80

DAY 38. **THE POWER OF FUTURE-FOCUSED**
WEALTH AND HEALTH 82

DAY 39. **THE POWER OF MINDSET IN LIFE'S**
UNEXPECTED MOMENTS 84

DAY 40. **REFRAMING YOUR MINDSET WITH**
THE STORY MODEL 86

DAY 41. **INTENTIONALITY AS A SUCCESS FACTOR** 88

DAY 42. **YOUR HEALTH** 90

DAY 43. **FOUR BUILDING BLOCKS OF FAITH** 92

DAY 44. **LEAVING A LEGACY** 94

DAY 45. **LEADING VS. ACCEPTING YOUR LIFE** 96

DAY 46. **BECOMING A ONE-PERCENTER** 98

DAY 47. **THE RANCH** 100

DAY 48. **CHILDHOOD TRAITS** 102

DAY 49. **DIVINE SURPRISES** 104

DAY 50. **HAVE YOU FILLED A BUCKET TODAY?** 106

DAY 51. **THE DISEASE OF DISTRACTION** 108

DAY 52. **THE GOOD LIST: PART 1** 110

DAY 53. **THE GOOD LIST: PART 2** 112

DAY 54. **THE GOOD LIST: PART 3** 114

DAY 55. **THE LAW OF INTENTIONALITY** 116

DAY 56. **MOTIVATIONS** 118

DAY 57. **SHAKE SALT AND SHINE LIGHT** 120

DAY 58. **EXTRAORDINARY LEADERSHIP** 122

DAY 59. **THE SECRET SAUCE: ASKING GREAT QUESTIONS** 124

DAY 60. **ROOTED** 126

DAY 61. **DETERMINE TO DO THE WORK** 128

DAY 62. **BREAK FREE FROM A FIXED MINDSET** 130

DAY 63. **FOCUS: PART 1** 132

DAY 64. **FOCUS: PART 2** 134

DAY 65. **FOCUS: PART 3** 136

DAY 66. **FOCUS: PART 4** 138

DAY 67. **YOUR BODY, HIS TEMPLE** 140

DAY 68. **OBEDIENCE OVER PERFORMANCE** 142

DAY 69. **BE WHERE YOUR FEET ARE** 144

DAY 70. **BEING A SECURE LEADER** 146

DAY 71. **BUILDING** 148

DAY 72. **BUILDERS** 150

DAY 73. **WHOSE JOB IS IT?** 152

DAY 74. **THREE LEADERSHIP MINDSETS: PART 1** 154

DAY 75. **THREE LEADERSHIP MINDSETS: PART 2** 156

DAY 76. **THREE LEADERSHIP MINDSETS: PART 3** 158

DAY 77. **POSSESSING PASSION** 160

DAY 78. **DEEP WORK** 162

DAY 79. **VISION FIRST, THEN VICTORY** 164

DAY 80. **ENTREPRENEURIAL KINGDOM WORK** 166

DAY 81. **LESSONS FROM WINSTON CHURCHILL** 168

DAY 82. **ADVICE FOR YOUNGER GENERATIONS** 170

DAY 83. **THE MONEY HABIT OF GENEROSITY** 172

DAY 84. **LESSONS FROM THE GREAT JOHN WESLEY** 174

DAY 85. **ALWAYS EXCEED EXPECTATIONS** 176

DAY 86. **CONSISTENCY IN LEADERSHIP** 178

DAY 87. **HOW TO *REAL* AND NOT WEIRD** 180

DAY 88. **THE THREE MUST-DOs** 182

DAY 89. **THE FOUR PICTURES OF GOD** 184

DAY 90. **BE A GREEN TAG PERSON** 186

A FRESH START

Intentional living maximizes your life!

REVIEW, REFLECT, AND RESPOND

As you read Day 1: "A Fresh Start" in *Restore: 90 Days of Intentional Living in Faith, Life, and Business*, review, reflect on, and respond to the text by answering the following question.

_____

When was the last time you set a clear intention and followed through with it until transformation occurred, and what did that process expose about your character or discipline?

_____

_____

_____

_____

_____

> *"For we are his workmanship, created in Christ Jesus for good works, which God prepared beforehand, that we should walk in them."*
>
> —*Ephesians 2:10 (ESV)*

Consider the scripture and answer the following question:

In what ways have you treated your "good works" as self-initiated goals rather than God-authored assignments?

_____

_____

_____

_____

_____

_____

_____

POWER OF MOMENTS

*There is so much for one to learn in
the powerful moments of life.*

REVIEW, REFLECT, AND RESPOND

As you read Day 2: "Power of Moments" in *Restore: 90 Days of Intentional Living in Faith, Life, and Business*, review, reflect on, and respond to the text by answering the following question.

What moments from the last year have most shaped who you are—and how do those moments reveal where God was teaching you wisdom?

_____

_____

_____

_____

_____

_____

"So teach us to number our days, that we may apply our hearts unto wisdom."

—*Psalm 90:12 (KJV)*

Consider the scripture and answer the following question:

When you reflect on your daily choices, do they reflect a heart of wisdom—or one of distraction and busyness?

_____

_____

_____

_____

_____

_____

WINNING: PART 1

*Interested people manage time, and
obsessed people manage focus.*

REVIEW, REFLECT, AND RESPOND

As you read Day 3: "Winning: Part 1" in *Restore: 90 Days of Intentional Living in Faith, Life, and Business*, review, reflect on, and respond to the text by answering the following question.

When have you allowed comfort or success to dull your passion for what once required your full focus?

_____

_____

_____

_____

_____

_____

"Do you not know that in a race all the runners run, but only one gets the prize? Run in such a way as to get the prize."

—*1 Corinthians 9:24 (NIV)*

Consider the scripture and answer the following question:

How does your current focus reflect someone running for a prize rather than for approval or survival?

_____

_____

_____

_____

_____

_____

WINNING: PART 2

The sacrifice to win is so much
bigger than everything else.

REVIEW, REFLECT, AND RESPOND

As you read Day 4: "Winning: Part 2" in *Restore: 90 Days of Intentional Living in Faith, Life, and Business*, review, reflect on, and respond to the text by answering the following question.

Which of the three winning principles—balance, emotional control, or sacrifice—do you most resist, and what does that resistance reveal about your maturity as a leader?

_____

_____

_____

_____

_____

_____

> *"Be wise in the way you act toward outsiders; make the most of every opportunity."*
>
> —*Colossians 4:5 (NIV)*

Consider the scripture and answer the following question:

What does it look like to "make the most" of every opportunity in your current season of leadership?

_____

_____

_____

_____

_____

PASSION

Do you care enough to endure, and not just start?

REVIEW, REFLECT, AND RESPOND

As you read Day 5: "Passion" in *Restore: 90 Days of Intentional Living in Faith, Life, and Business*, review, reflect on, and respond to the text by answering the following question.

When have you been excited but unwilling to suffer for the outcome—and how has that pattern limited your impact?

_____

_____

_____

_____

_____

_____

> *"Their hearts are like an oven; they approach him with intrigue. Their passion smolders all night; in the morning it blazes like a flaming fire."*
>
> —Hosea 7:6 (NIV)

Consider the scripture and answer the following question:

What would it require for your passion to move from emotional intensity to sacrificial endurance?

_____

_____

_____

_____

_____

_____

PRESSURE

When pressure confines you, it will shrink you.

REVIEW, REFLECT, AND RESPOND

As you read Day 6: "Pressure" in *Restore: 90 Days of Intentional Living in Faith, Life, and Business*, review, reflect on, and respond to the text by answering the following question.

How does your leadership culture handle stress—through control or through faith?

_____

_____

_____

_____

_____

_____

> *"Consider it pure joy, my brothers and sisters, whenever you face trials of many kinds, because you know that the testing of your faith produces perseverance."*
>
> —James 1:2–3 (NIV)

Consider the scripture and answer the following question:

What current test is producing perseverance in you if you'll allow it?

_____

_____

_____

_____

_____

_____

_____

INVESTMENT MINDSET

*Investing in yourself and others
is sowing good seed.*

REVIEW, REFLECT, AND RESPOND

As you read Day 7: "Investment Mindset" in *Restore: 90 Days of Intentional Living in Faith, Life, and Business*, review, reflect on, and respond to the text by answering the following question.

What "expense mindset" belief still keeps you from pouring into people or projects that yield eternal dividends?

_____

_____

_____

_____

_____

> *"A man reaps what he sows. . . . Let us not become weary in doing good, for at the proper time we will reap a harvest if we do not give up."*
>
> —*Galatians 6:7–9 (NIV)*

Consider the scripture and answer the following questions:

What are you currently sowing into your business or relationships that will determine next season's harvest? What are you tempted to give up because the return isn't instant?

_____

_____

_____

_____

_____

_____

TWO TYPES
OF PEOPLE

*You get to choose which type of
person you want to be!*

REVIEW, REFLECT, AND RESPOND

As you read Day 8: "Two Types of People" in *Restore: 90 Days of Intentional Living in Faith, Life, and Business*, review, reflect on, and respond to the text by answering the following question.

Which list—"people who make things happen" or "people who wait"—most describes you right now, and why?

_____

_____

_____

_____

_____

_____

> *"Now that you know these things, you will be blessed if you do them."*
>
> —*John 13:17 (NIV)*

Consider the scripture and answer the following question:

In what area of life are you waiting for movement when God is waiting for action?

_____

_____

_____

_____

_____

_____

MISSING THE MARK

*Sometimes, what you thought would make
you happy makes you feel empty.*

REVIEW, REFLECT, AND RESPOND

As you read Day 9: "Missing the Mark" in *Restore: 90 Days of Intentional Living in Faith, Life, and Business*, review, reflect on, and respond to the text by answering the following question.

Where have you mistaken freedom for permission—and how has that led to emptiness instead of joy?

_____

_____

_____

_____

_____

_____

> *"Therefore, if anyone is in Christ, the new creation has come: The old has gone, the new is here!"*
>
> —2 Corinthians 5:17 (NIV)

Consider the scripture and answer the following question:

What "old" habits or thought patterns are keeping you from walking in your new identity?

_____

_____

_____

_____

_____

_____

_____

CONTENTMENT

Walking with the Holy Spirit gives you more of the YOU that God created you to be.

REVIEW, REFLECT, AND RESPOND

As you read Day 10: "Contentment" in *Restore: 90 Days of Intentional Living in Faith, Life, and Business*, review, reflect on, and respond to the text by answering the following question.

Which of the six contentment checkpoints—framework, authority, time, hardship, empathy, relationship—revealed a growth area for you?

_____

_____

_____

_____

_____

_____

"And we know that in all things God works for the good of those who love him, who have been called according to his purpose."

—Romans 8:28 (NIV)

Consider the scripture and answer the following question:

What evidence of God's redemptive work have you overlooked because it didn't fit your timeline?

_____

_____

_____

_____

_____

_____

_____

PERSPECTIVE

Change of Place + Change of Pace =
Change in Perspective

REVIEW, REFLECT, AND RESPOND

As you read Day 11: "Perspective" in *Restore: 90 Days of Intentional Living in Faith, Life, and Business*, review, reflect on, and respond to the text by answering the following question.

What environment most helps you see clearly again, and how can you schedule it regularly?

_____

_____

_____

_____

_____

_____

"The eye is the lamp of the body. If your eyes are healthy, your whole body will be full of light."

—*Matthew 6:22 (NIV)*

Consider the scripture and answer the following question:

What are you allowing your eyes—your focus—to dwell on daily, and how is it shaping your inner world?

_____

_____

_____

_____

_____

_____

THE FIVE Ps OF SUCCESS

*Your attitude is the only thing that
you get to choose every day.*

REVIEW, REFLECT, AND RESPOND

As you read Day 12: "The Five Ps of Success" in *Restore: 90 Days of Intentional Living in Faith, Life, and Business*, review, reflect on, and respond to the text by answering the following question.

Which "P" do you need to cultivate this week, and what daily habit could strengthen it?

_____

_____

_____

_____

_____

> *"Rejoice in the Lord always. I will say it again: Rejoice. Let your gentleness be evident to all. The Lord is near. Do not be anxious about anything, but in every situation, by prayer and petition, with thanksgiving, present your requests to God."*
>
> —*Philippians 4:4–6 (NIV)*

Consider the scripture and answer the following question:

What might "gentleness evident to all" look like in your leadership today?

_____

_____

_____

_____

_____

_____

THE FOUR Cs

When faced with fear, you have two choices: you can avoid it, or you can have the courage to push through.

REVIEW, REFLECT, AND RESPOND

As you read Day 13: "The Four Cs" in *Restore: 90 Days of Intentional Living in Faith, Life, and Business*, review, reflect on, and respond to the text by answering the following question.

———————————————————————————

How has fear disguised itself as logic when God asked you to commit to something risky?

_____

_____

_____

_____

_____

_____

"You and these people who come to you will only wear yourselves out. The work is too heavy for you; you cannot handle it alone."

—Exodus 18:18 (NIV)

Consider the scripture and answer the following question:

Where are you refusing help because you equate independence with strength?

_____

_____

_____

_____

_____

_____

_____

THINKING HIGHER

Don't just address the symptoms of the problem, but get to the actual root.

REVIEW, REFLECT, AND RESPOND

As you read Day 14: "Thinking Higher" in *Restore: 90 Days of Intentional Living in Faith, Life, and Business*, review, reflect on, and respond to the text by answering the following question.

What situation are you too close to emotionally, and how is it clouding your leadership judgment?

_____

_____

_____

_____

_____

_____

> *"What do you know that we do not know? What insights do you have that we do not have?"*
>
> —Job 15:9 (NIV)

Consider the scripture and answer the following question:

What new insight that you didn't have before is God trying to reveal that requires emotional distance to perceive?

_____

_____

_____

_____

_____

_____

YOUR UNIQUENESS

I became intentional in everything,
and because of that,
my life grew exponentially!

REVIEW, REFLECT, AND RESPOND

As you read Day 15: "Your Uniqueness" in *Restore: 90 Days of Intentional Living in Faith, Life, and Business*, review, reflect on, and respond to the text by answering the following question.

What problem do you solve because of what you've personally overcome?

_____

_____

_____

_____

_____

_____

> "And even the very hairs of your head are all numbered. So don't be afraid; you are worth more than many sparrows."
>
> —*Matthew 10:30–31 (NIV)*

Consider the scripture and answer the following question:

Where has fear caused you to downplay or copy others instead of owning your uniqueness?

_____

_____

_____

_____

_____

_____

_____

BEING A GIVER

*If you are breathing, you need encouragement
and help in some area of your life.*

REVIEW, REFLECT, AND RESPOND

As you read Day 16: "Being a Giver" in *Restore: 90 Days of Intentional Living in Faith, Life, and Business*, review, reflect on, and respond to the text by answering the following question.

What habit or rhythm could you establish to practice intentional generosity—like keeping a "gift ideas" list on your phone?

_____

_____

_____

_____

_____

_____

> *"Each of you should give what you have decided in your heart to give, not reluctantly or under compulsion, for God loves a cheerful giver*
>
> —*2 Corinthians 9:7 (NIV)*

Consider the scripture and answer the following question:

How has reluctance or fear ever limited your generosity toward people, causes, or opportunities?

_____

_____

_____

_____

_____

_____

SERVING

The path to peace is service!

REVIEW, REFLECT, AND RESPOND

As you read Day 17: "Serving" in *Restore: 90 Days of Intentional Living in Faith, Life, and Business*, review, reflect on, and respond to the text by answering the following question.

How do you define "success" in your leadership—and how does that definition include service?

_____

_____

_____

_____

_____

_____

> *"For even the Son of Man did not come to be served, but to serve."*
>
> —*Mark 10:45 (NIV)*

Consider the scripture and answer the following question:

When was the last time you prioritized someone's needs above your own mission or profit?

_____

_____

_____

_____

_____

_____

_____

YOUR BEST DECADE EVER

*What do you want the next ten
years of your life to look like?*

REVIEW, REFLECT, AND RESPOND

As you read Day 18: "Your Best Decade Ever" in *Restore: 90 Days of Intentional Living in Faith, Life, and Business*, review, reflect on, and respond to the text by answering the following question.

Which category—creativity, health, or family—requires the most intentional growth in this next decade? Write a plan outlining specific goals, habits, and milestones that will move you toward growth in that area.

_____

_____

_____

_____

_____

"This is what the LORD says—your Redeemer, the Holy One of Israel: 'I am the LORD your God, who teaches you what is best for you, who directs you in the way you should go.'"

—Isaiah 48:17 (NIV)

Consider the scripture and answer the following question:

In what area of your life has God been teaching you "what is best," and how have you responded?

_____

_____

_____

_____

_____

THRIVE IN A DOWNTURN

Just do something.

REVIEW, REFLECT, AND RESPOND

As you read Day 19: "Thrive in a Downturn" in *Restore: 90 Days of Intentional Living in Faith, Life, and Business*, review, reflect on, and respond to the text by answering the following question.

In this season, what mindset do you need to renew, which relationships do you need to invest in, and what action do you need to take so that you can thrive—not just endure—where God has placed you?

_____

_____

_____

_____

_____

_____

> *"May the LORD, the God of your ancestors, increase you a thousand times and bless you as he has promised!"*
>
> —*Deuteronomy 1:11 (NIV)*

Consider the scripture and answer the following question:

What does this blessing mean for how you face seasons of scarcity or downturn?

_____

_____

_____

_____

_____

_____

THE BEST OF THE BEST

*The best of the best are always
looking to get better.*

REVIEW, REFLECT, AND RESPOND

As you read Day 20: "The Best of the Best" in *Restore: 90 Days of Intentional Living in Faith, Life, and Business*, review, reflect on, and respond to the text by answering the following question.

Who models "the best of the best" in your field, and what disciplines set them apart?

_____

_____

_____

_____

_____

_____

"Whatever you do, do all to the glory of God."

—*1 Corinthians 10:31 (NIV)*

Consider the scripture and answer the following question:

In what area of your life or leadership have you settled for good instead of God-glorifying great?

_____

_____

_____

_____

_____

_____

HAPPINESS

Happiness is much like success. . . .
You don't find it; you create it.

REVIEW, REFLECT, AND RESPOND

As you read Day 21: "Happiness" in *Restore: 90 Days of Intentional Living in Faith, Life, and Business*, review, reflect on, and respond to the text by answering the following question.

Where have you confused happiness with comfort, and how is God redefining both?

_____

_____

_____

_____

_____

_____

"Finally, brothers and sisters, whatever is true, whatever is noble, whatever is right, whatever is pure, whatever is lovely, whatever is admirable—if anything is excellent or praiseworthy—think about such things."

—*Philippians 4:8 (NIV)*

Consider the scripture and answer the following question:

Which distractions or influences consistently steal your joy?

_____

_____

_____

_____

_____

_____

LEADERSHIP TOOLKIT

All great leaders serve others.

REVIEW, REFLECT, AND RESPOND

As you read Day 22: "Leadership Toolkit" in *Restore: 90 Days of Intentional Living in Faith, Life, and Business*, review, reflect on, and respond to the text by answering the following question.

Which "tool" from your leadership kit (service, self-care, succession, or development) needs sharpening most right now, and what changes will you make to sharpen it?

_____

_____

_____

_____

_____

_____

"May his days be few; may another take his place of leadership."

—*Psalm 109:8 (NIV)*

Consider the scripture and answer the following question:

What systems or people are you preparing to "take your place" someday?

_____

_____

_____

_____

_____

_____

THE FIVE WELLS OF A MOREHOUSE MAN

Well-spoken means not opening your mouth before you know something.

REVIEW, REFLECT, AND RESPOND

As you read Day 23: "The Five Wells of a Morehouse Man" in *Restore: 90 Days of Intentional Living in Faith, Life, and Business*, review, reflect on, and respond to the text by answering the following question.

Which of the Five Wells—well-read, well-spoken, well-dressed, well-traveled, or well-balanced—most needs your attention, and how has neglecting one of these areas limited your leadership credibility?

_____

_____

_____

_____

_____

_____

"From the fruit of their lips people are filled with good things, and the work of their hands brings them reward."

—*Proverbs 12:14 (NIV)*

Consider the scripture and answer the following question:

How are your words currently bearing fruit—are they building up or tearing down?

_____

_____

_____

_____

_____

A REVERENCE

Pioneers break ground; they never build the greatest, but they inspire people to build the greatest because of their love and respect for what they do.

REVIEW, REFLECT, AND RESPOND

As you read Day 24: "A Reverence" in *Restore: 90 Days of Intentional Living in Faith, Life, and Business*, review, reflect on, and respond to the text by answering the following question.

What small act of love or excellence could restore awe in your daily work?

_____

_____

_____

_____

_____

_____

> *"Whatever you do, work at it with all your heart, as working for the Lord, not for human masters."*
>
> —*Colossians 3:23 (NIV)*

Consider the scripture and answer the following question:

Where have you allowed routine to replace reverence in your leadership or calling?

_____

_____

_____

_____

_____

_____

_____

WHY NOT YOU?

Doing hard things actually strengthens you.

REVIEW, REFLECT, AND RESPOND

As you read Day 25: "Why Not You?" in *Restore: 90 Days of Intentional Living in Faith, Life, and Business*, review, reflect on, and respond to the text by answering the following question.

What fear has kept you from pursuing something bold, and what truth could replace it?

_____

_____

_____

_____

_____

> *"Jesus looked at them and said, 'With man this is impossible, but with God all things are possible.'"*
>
> —*Matthew 19:26 (NIV)*

Consider the scripture and answer the following question:

What dream or assignment feels impossible right now, and how does this verse reframe what's actually possible in your situation?

_____

_____

_____

_____

_____

_____

SEVEN INTENTIONAL LUNCH QUESTIONS

*Every month, you should have at least one lunch
with someone bigger and better than you.*

REVIEW, REFLECT, AND RESPOND

As you read Day 26: "Seven Intentional Lunch Questions" in *Restore: 90 Days of Intentional Living in Faith, Life, and Business*, review, reflect on, and respond to the text by answering the following question.

Who could you invite to lunch this month that might change how you think and lead?

_____

_____

_____

_____

_____

_____

> *"Remember your leaders, who spoke the word of God to you. Consider the outcome of their way of life and imitate their faith."*
>
> —*Hebrews 13:7 (NIV)*

Consider the scripture and answer the following question:

Who has modeled the kind of faith and leadership you want to imitate?

_____

_____

_____

_____

_____

_____

_____

PERSONAL DEFINITION OF SUCCESS

We are wired to do what we are passionate about.

REVIEW, REFLECT, AND RESPOND

As you read Day 27: "Personal Definition of Success" in *Restore: 90 Days of Intentional Living in Faith, Life, and Business*, review, reflect on, and respond to the text by answering the following question.

Which of your passions and strengths most clearly reflect the purpose God designed you for?

_____

_____

_____

_____

_____

_____

"Each of you should use whatever gift you have received to serve others, as faithful stewards of God's grace in its various forms."

—*1 Peter 4:10 (NIV)*

Consider the scripture and answer the following question:

What area of your leadership most needs to be realigned with stewardship instead of striving?

_____

_____

_____

_____

_____

_____

_____

WISDOM

*The only problem you will really ever
have is a wisdom problem.*

REVIEW, REFLECT, AND RESPOND

As you read Day 28: "Wisdom" in *Restore: 90 Days of Intentional Living in Faith, Life, and Business*, review, reflect on, and respond to the text by answering the following question.

How have past seasons of ignorance produced avoidable pain, and what did you learn?

_____

_____

_____

_____

_____

"Let the wise listen and add to their learning, and let the discerning get guidance."

—Proverbs 1:5 (NIV)

Consider the scripture and answer the following question:

What voices are currently shaping your discernment—for better or worse?

_____

_____

_____

_____

_____

_____

JOY

Joy is to be released, not reserved.

REVIEW, REFLECT, AND RESPOND

As you read Day 29: "Joy" in *Restore: 90 Days of Intentional Living in Faith, Life, and Business*, review, reflect on, and respond to the text by answering the following question.

When was the last time you felt genuine joy in your work, and what produced it?

_____

_____

_____

_____

_____

_____

_____

"Do not grieve, for the joy of the LORD is your strength."

—*Nehemiah 8:10 (NIV)*

Consider the scripture and answer the following question:

What threatens to drain your joy most quickly, and how can you guard against it?

_____

_____

_____

_____

_____

_____

_____

OBEDIENCE

Promotion always follows obedience.

REVIEW, REFLECT, AND RESPOND

As you read Day 30: "Obedience" in *Restore: 90 Days of Intentional Living in Faith, Life, and Business*, review, reflect on, and respond to the text by answering the following question.

What small act of obedience today could open the door to greater purpose tomorrow?

_____

_____

_____

_____

_____

_____

"If you are willing and obedient, you will eat the best from the land."

—Isaiah 1:19 (NIV)

Consider the scripture and answer the following question:

Where have you been willing but not obedient—or obedient but not willing?

_____

_____

_____

_____

_____

_____

_____

CHOICES

You're either preparing yourself for the next opportunity or robbing yourself of it based on the decision you make.

REVIEW, REFLECT, AND RESPOND

As you read Day 31: "Choices" in *Restore: 90 Days of Intentional Living in Faith, Life, and Business*, review, reflect on, and respond to the text by answering the following question.

Which recurring choice most determines the quality of your outcomes right now?

_____

_____

_____

_____

_____

_____

> *"But if serving the LORD seems undesirable to you, then choose for yourselves this day whom you will serve. . . . But as for me and my house, we will serve the LORD."*
>
> —*Joshua 24:15 (NIV)*

Consider the scripture and answer the following question:

How does your daily decision-making reveal whom you truly serve?

_____

_____

_____

_____

_____

_____

_____

BE A COFFEE BEAN

Life is like a pot of boiling water.

REVIEW, REFLECT, AND RESPOND

As you read Day 32: "Be a Coffee Bean" in *Restore: 90 Days of Intentional Living in Faith, Life, and Business*, review, reflect on, and respond to the text by answering the following question.

In recent challenges, have you responded more like a carrot, an egg, or a coffee bean, and why?

_____

_____

_____

_____

_____

"Whoever walks with the wise becomes wise, but the companion of fools will suffer harm."

—*Proverbs 13:20 (author paraphrase)*

Consider the scripture and answer the following question:

What does the company you keep say about whether you should change your environment or conform to it?

_____

_____

_____

_____

_____

_____

INCREASING YOUR CAPACITY FOR STRESS

Stress happens when pressure exceeds capacity.

REVIEW, REFLECT, AND RESPOND

As you read Day 33: "Increasing Your Capacity for Stress" in *Restore: 90 Days of Intentional Living in Faith, Life, and Business*, review, reflect on, and respond to the text by answering the following question.

Which area—rest, identity, purpose, relationships, or faith—needs strengthening to handle pressure well?

_____

_____

_____

_____

_____

_____

> *"Come to me, all you who are weary and burdened, and I will give you rest."*
>
> —*Matthew 11:28 (NIV)*

Consider the scripture and answer the following question:

What burdens have you been carrying alone instead of bringing to Jesus?

_____

_____

_____

_____

_____

_____

_____

BECOMING THE YOU OF YOUR INDUSTRY

Stop competing and start creating!

REVIEW, REFLECT, AND RESPOND

As you read Day 34: "Becoming the You of Your Industry" in *Restore: 90 Days of Intentional Living in Faith, Life, and Business*, review, reflect on, and respond to the text by answering the following question.

How are you creating experiences that make people feel valued, not just served?

_____

_____

_____

_____

_____

_____

"Do not conform to the pattern of this world, but be transformed by the renewing of your mind."

—*Romans 12:2 (NIV)*

Consider the scripture and answer the following question:

Where are you tempted to conform to the patterns of your industry instead of innovating?

_____

_____

_____

_____

_____

_____

_____

NEVER SPLIT THE DIFFERENCE: THE POWER OF NEGOTIATION

In business and life, we often compromise too quickly.

REVIEW, REFLECT, AND RESPOND

As you read Day 35: "Never Split the Difference: The Power of Negotiation" in *Restore: 90 Days of Intentional Living in Faith, Life, and Business*, review, reflect on, and respond to the text by answering the following question.

When do you tend to "split the difference" instead of seeking true understanding?

_____

_____

_____

_____

_____

_____

> *"The heart of the wise makes his speech judicious and adds persuasiveness to his lips."*
>
> —*Proverbs 16:23 (ESV)*

Consider the scripture and answer the following question:

What does this verse teach you about balancing empathy and authority when communicating?

_____

_____

_____

_____

_____

_____

_____

BECOMING YOUR FUTURE SELF

Your future is not dictated by your past—
it is pulled forward by your vision.

REVIEW, REFLECT, AND RESPOND

As you read Day 36: "Becoming Your Future Self" in *Restore: 90 Days of Intentional Living in Faith, Life, and Business*, review, reflect on, and respond to the text by answering the following question.

What decision today would your future self thank you for?

_____

_____

_____

_____

_____

_____

"Where there is no vision, the people perish."

—Proverbs 29:18 (KJV)

Consider the scripture and answer the following question:

What future are you currently believing God for—and are your habits aligned with it?

_____

_____

_____

_____

_____

_____

_____

THE SIX HUMAN NEEDS: UNDERSTANDING WHAT DRIVES YOU

True fulfillment comes from growing and giving.

REVIEW, REFLECT, AND RESPOND

As you read Day 37: "The Six Human Needs: Understanding
What Drives You" in *Restore: 90 Days of Intentional Living
in Faith, Life, and Business*, review, reflect on, and respond
to the text by answering the following question.

What would faithful stewardship of your unique gifts look like in this
next season of leadership and life?

_____

_____

_____

_____

_____

_____

*"Each of you should use whatever gift you have received to serve
others, as faithful stewards of God's grace in its various forms."*

—1 Peter 4:10 (NIV)

Consider the scripture and answer the following question:

In what ways might you be using your abilities for self-fulfillment rather
than stewardship?

_____

_____

_____

_____

_____

_____

THE POWER OF FUTURE-FOCUSED WEALTH AND HEALTH

*The wealthiest and healthiest people
don't let life happen to them.*

REVIEW, REFLECT, AND RESPOND

As you read Day 38: "The Power of Future-Focused Wealth and Health" in *Restore: 90 Days of Intentional Living in Faith, Life, and Business*, review, reflect on, and respond to the text by answering the following question.

List three people or mentors you need in your circle to help you stay diligent and disciplined. What intentional effort will you make this week to build relationships with them?

_____

_____

_____

_____

_____

_____

"The plans of the diligent lead surely to abundance, but everyone who is hasty comes only to poverty."

—*Proverbs 21:5 (ESV)*

Consider the scripture and answer the following question:

Which of your plans requires more patience and intentionality before it can bear fruit?

_____

_____

_____

_____

_____

_____

THE POWER OF MINDSET IN LIFE'S UNEXPECTED MOMENTS

Your mindset is the foundation of your resilience—strengthen it before life tests you.

REVIEW, REFLECT, AND RESPOND

As you read Day 39: "The Power of Mindset in Life's Unexpected Moments" in *Restore: 90 Days of Intentional Living in Faith, Life, and Business*, review, reflect on, and respond to the text by answering the following question.

What daily thought habit could help you remain grounded in peace regardless of circumstances?

_____

_____

_____

_____

_____

_____

> *"So do not fear, for I am with you; do not be dismayed, for I am your God. I will strengthen you and help you; I will uphold you with my righteous right hand."*
>
> —*Isaiah 41:10 (NIV)*

Consider the scripture and answer the following question:

How does God's promise to strengthen and uphold you reshape the way you handle unexpected challenges?

_____

_____

_____

_____

_____

REFRAMING YOUR MINDSET WITH THE STORY MODEL

Your mind will always seek evidence to confirm the story you tell yourself.

REVIEW, REFLECT, AND RESPOND

As you read Day 40: "Reframing Your Mindset with the Story Model" in *Restore: 90 Days of Intentional Living in Faith, Life, and Business*, review, reflect on, and respond to the text by answering the following question.

What "story" have you been telling yourself that may not be true—and how could reframing it set you free?

_____

_____

_____

_____

_____

_____

"Love bears all things, believes all things, hopes all things, endures all things."

—*I Corinthians 13:7 (ESV)*

Consider the scripture and answer the following question:

How does love influence the way you interpret the "stories" you tell yourself about others?

_____

_____

_____

_____

_____

_____

_____

INTENTIONALITY AS A SUCCESS FACTOR

*You can learn accidentally,
or you can learn intentionally.*

REVIEW, REFLECT, AND RESPOND

As you read Day 41: "Intentionality as a Success Factor" in *Restore: 90 Days of Intentional Living in Faith, Life, and Business*, review, reflect on, and respond to the text by answering the following question.

What was the last environment or person that stretched your thinking and growth, and how can you intentionally recreate that kind of stretching environment in your current season so growth becomes a consistent rhythm, not an accident?

_____

_____

_____

_____

_____

_____

> *"Always remember what you have been taught, and don't let go of it. Keep all that you have learned; it is the most important thing in life."*
>
> —*Proverbs 4:13 (author paraphrase)*

Consider the scripture and answer the following question:

What principles or lessons have you neglected that need to be reactivated in your life?

_____

_____

_____

_____

_____

_____

YOUR HEALTH

The reality is, if we don't fight for our bodies and our health, no one else will.

REVIEW, REFLECT, AND RESPOND

As you read Day 42: "Your Health" in *Restore: 90 Days of Intentional Living in Faith, Life, and Business*, review, reflect on, and respond to the text by answering the following question.

Which part of your daily routine most affects your physical or spiritual energy (either for better or for worse)?

_____

_____

_____

_____

_____

> *"Or do you not know that your body is a temple of the Holy Spirit within you, whom you have from God? You are not your own, for you were bought with a price. So glorify God in your body."*
>
> —*1 Corinthians 6:19-20 (ESV)*

Consider the scripture and answer the following question:

Where have you been careless or disconnected from stewardship of your health?

_____

_____

_____

_____

_____

_____

_____

FOUR BUILDING BLOCKS OF FAITH

It is your faith and belief system that FUELS you as a believer.

REVIEW, REFLECT, AND RESPOND

As you read Day 43: "Four Building Blocks of Faith" in *Restore: 90 Days of Intentional Living in Faith, Life, and Business*, review, reflect on, and respond to the text by answering the following question.

Which of the four building blocks—intimacy with God, community, obedience, or sharing your faith—needs your attention most, and why is it the most difficult for you?

_____

_____

_____

_____

_____

_____

"For we live by faith, not by sight."

—*2 Corinthians 5:7 (NIV)*

Consider the scripture and answer the following question:

What step of obedience is God asking of you before you see results?

_____

_____

_____

_____

_____

_____

_____

LEAVING A LEGACY

If you want to leave a legacy as a leader, you've got to be thinking BIG and thinking intentionally.

REVIEW, REFLECT, AND RESPOND

As you read Day 44: "Leaving a Legacy" in *Restore: 90 Days of Intentional Living in Faith, Life, and Business*, review, reflect on, and respond to the text by answering the following question.

What "big bucket" items would force you to depend on God instead of your ability?

_____

_____

_____

_____

_____

> *"Now to him who is able to do immeasurably more than all we ask or imagine, according to his power that is at work within us, to him be glory in the church and in Christ Jesus throughout all generations, for ever and ever! Amen."*
>
> *—Ephesians 3:20–21 (NIV)*

Consider the scripture and answer the following question:

In what ways would believing in God's immeasurable power expand your vision for legacy? Be specific.

_____

_____

_____

_____

_____

_____

LEADING VS. ACCEPTING YOUR LIFE

Most people don't lead their lives; they
accept their lives, and an accepted
life is an unintentional life.

REVIEW, REFLECT, AND RESPOND

As you read Day 45: "Leading vs. Accepting Your Life" in *Restore: 90 Days of Intentional Living in Faith, Life, and Business*, review, reflect on, and respond to the text by answering the following question.

What decision could you make this week that shifts you from survival mode to leadership mode?

_____

_____

_____

_____

_____

"Show me the right path, O LORD; point out the road for me to follow. Lead me by your truth and teach me, for you are the God who saves me. All day long I put my hope in you."

—Psalm 25:4–5 (NLT)

Consider the scripture and answer the following question:

Where have you been passively accepting circumstances instead of leading through them with faith?

_____

_____

_____

_____

_____

_____

BECOMING A ONE-PERCENTER

One percenters are rare.

REVIEW, REFLECT, AND RESPOND

As you read Day 46: "Becoming a One-Percenter" in *Restore: 90 Days of Intentional Living in Faith, Life, and Business*, review, reflect on, and respond to the text by answering the following question.

What does being a one percenter for God's glory—not your own—look like in your current role?

_____

_____

_____

_____

> *"Whatever you do, work at it with all your heart, as working for the Lord, not for human masters, since you know that you will receive an inheritance from the Lord as a reward. It is the Lord Christ you are serving."*
>
> —*Colossians 3:23–24*

Consider the scripture and answer the following question:

Where might half-hearted effort be signaling misplaced focus or fatigue, and how can you invite God into that space to restore purpose?

_____

_____

_____

_____

_____

_____

THE RANCH

It was one small, yet intentional act on my part.

REVIEW, REFLECT, AND RESPOND

As you read Day 47: "The Ranch" in *Restore: 90 Days of Intentional Living in Faith, Life, and Business*, review, reflect on, and respond to the text by answering the following question.

When has a single small act of intentionality produced unexpected influence or favor?

_____

_____

_____

_____

_____

_____

> *"All hard work brings a profit, but mere talk leads only to poverty."*
>
> —*Proverbs 14:23 (NIV)*

Consider the scripture and answer the following question:

Where have you been talking about impact instead of taking the next faithful step?

_____

_____

_____

_____

_____

_____

_____

CHILDHOOD TRAITS

Have you discovered what your gifts are?

REVIEW, REFLECT, AND RESPOND

As you read Day 48: "Childhood Traits" in *Restore: 90 Days of Intentional Living in Faith, Life, and Business*, review, reflect on, and respond to the text by answering the following question.

What new space or opportunity could become a platform for your unique gifts to glorify God?

_____

_____

_____

_____

_____

_____

"Each of you should use whatever gift you have received to serve others, as faithful stewards of God's grace."

—1 Peter 4:10 (NIV)

Consider the scripture and answer the following question:

How do your earliest passions and traits reflect the gifts God planted in you from birth?

_____

_____

_____

_____

_____

_____

_____

DIVINE SURPRISES

You don't have to chase the blessings or surprises. If you chase God, the blessings and surprises will chase you!

REVIEW, REFLECT, AND RESPOND

As you read Day 49: "Divine Surprises" in *Restore: 90 Days of Intentional Living in Faith, Life, and Business*, review, reflect on, and respond to the text by answering the following question.

Write down one situation where you've been waiting for a breakthrough. What would it look like to thank God in advance for the divine surprise?

_____

_____

_____

_____

> "If you listen obediently to the Voice of GOD, your God, and heartily obey all of his commandments that I command you today, GOD, your God, will place you on high, high above all the nations and worlds. All these blessings will come down on you and spread out beyond you because you have responded to the Voice of GOD."
>
> —Deuteronomy 28:1–3 (MSG)

Consider the scripture and answer the following question:

What step of obedience could you take today that demonstrates your trust that God sees and rewards faithfulness?

_____

_____

_____

_____

_____

HAVE YOU FILLED A BUCKET TODAY?

I want to fill someone's bucket every day.

REVIEW, REFLECT, AND RESPOND

As you read Day 50: "Have You Filled a Bucket Today?" in *Restore: 90 Days of Intentional Living in Faith, Life, and Business*, review, reflect on, and respond to the text by answering the following question.

Create a recurring reminder that simply says, "Fill a bucket." How will you use it to track your daily acts of encouragement?

_____

_____

_____

_____

_____

_____

"A generous person will prosper; whoever refreshes others will be refreshed."

—Proverbs 11:25 (NIV)

Consider the scripture and answer the following question:

Who in your life most needs encouragement right now, and how will you refresh them before the day ends?

_____

_____

_____

_____

_____

_____

_____

THE DISEASE OF DISTRACTION

The more influence you carry, the more intentional the enemy becomes in his strategy.

REVIEW, REFLECT, AND RESPOND

As you read Day 51: "The Disease of Distraction" in *Restore: 90 Days of Intentional Living in Faith, Life, and Business*, review, reflect on, and respond to the text by answering the following question.

Conduct a "distraction audit" tonight: list your top three distractions and the cost each one has created. What is your plan for eliminating them?

_____

_____

_____

_____

_____

_____

"Be still, and know that I am God."

—*Psalm 46:10 (NIV)*

Consider the scripture and answer the following question:

What boundary—time, device, or environment—do you need to establish to protect your stillness and position yourself to hear God's voice?

_____

_____

_____

_____

_____

_____

THE GOOD LIST: PART 1

*God is good all the time, and all
the time, God is good.*

REVIEW, REFLECT, AND RESPOND

As you read Day 52: "The Good List: Part 1" in *Restore: 90 Days of Intentional Living in Faith, Life, and Business*, review, reflect on, and respond to the text by answering the following question.

If you could write one action statement beginning with "Today I will . . ." that aligns with goodness, knowledge, and self-control, what would it be?

_____

_____

_____

_____

> *"Make every effort to add to your faith goodness; and to goodness, knowledge; and to knowledge, self-control. For if you possess these qualities in increasing measure, they will keep you from being ineffective and unproductive in your knowledge of our Lord Jesus Christ."*
>
> —*2 Peter 1:5 (NIV)*

Consider the scripture and answer the following question:

What would it look like today to let your understanding of God (knowledge) shape your reactions (self-control) and your treatment (goodness) of others?

_____

_____

_____

_____

_____

THE GOOD LIST: PART 2

*Little leads to much, and sustained
progress is little by little.*

REVIEW, REFLECT, AND RESPOND

As you read Day 53: "The Good List: Part 2" in *Restore: 90 Days of Intentional Living in Faith, Life, and Business*, review, reflect on, and respond to the text by answering the following question.

List one way you'll demonstrate perseverance in an ongoing challenge (specific action, not attitude).

_____

_____

_____

_____

_____

_____

> *"Make every effort to add to your faith perseverance, godliness, and mutual affection."*
>
> —1 Peter 1:6–7 (NIV)

Consider the scripture and answer the following question:

Who can you intentionally bless today who cannot return the favor—an act of true mutual affection?

_____

_____

_____

_____

_____

_____

THE GOOD LIST: PART 3

We have to be so deeply rooted in our faith
that even the hardest-to-love people
don't change who we are or our energy.

REVIEW, REFLECT, AND RESPOND

As you read Day 54: "The Good List: Part 3" in *Restore: 90 Days of Intentional Living in Faith, Life, and Business*, review, reflect on, and respond to the text by answering the following question.

Is your leadership or business known more for love or for achievement, and what intentional change could you make today to ensure love defines your influence more than success does?

_____

_____

_____

_____

> *"Make every effort to add to your faith goodness, knowledge, self-control, godliness, mutual affection, and love. For if you possess these qualities in increasing measure, they will keep you from being ineffective and unproductive in your knowledge of our Lord Jesus Christ."*
>
> —*2 Peter 1:5–8 (NIV, emphasis added)*

Consider the scripture and answer the following question:

Who is the "hard-to-love" person God is asking you to show grace to this week, and what concrete act of kindness will you take toward that person in the next 48 hours?

_____

_____

_____

_____

_____

THE LAW OF INTENTIONALITY

Growth isn't automatic. You have to go out of your way to find growth opportunities.

REVIEW, REFLECT, AND RESPOND

As you read Day 55: "The Law of Intentionality" in *Restore: 90 Days of Intentional Living in Faith, Life, and Business*, review, reflect on, and respond to the text by answering the following question.

Write one goal and set a visible deadline that forces you to move from intention to execution. Who will you tell about this goal so they can help hold you accountable to take action?

_____

_____

_____

_____

_____

"Do you not know that in a race all the runners run, but only one gets the prize? Run in such a way as to get the prize. Everyone who competes . . . goes into strict training."

—2 Corinthians 5:17 (NIV)

Consider the scripture and answer the following question:

What "finish line" are you aiming for in this season, and how will you know you're running in the right direction?

_____

_____

_____

_____

_____

_____

_____

MOTIVATIONS

You were created to live in "order"—in both nature and in how you live, worship, and lead.

REVIEW, REFLECT, AND RESPOND

As you read Day 56: "Motivations" in *Restore: 90 Days of Intentional Living in Faith, Life, and Business*, review, reflect on, and respond to the text by answering the following question.

What space (physical, relational, or spiritual) in your life is currently disordered, and what steps can you take to organize it as an act of worship?

_____

_____

_____

_____

_____

_____

> *"For in him all things were created . . . all things have been created through him and for him."*
>
> —*Colossians 1:16 (NIV)*

Consider the scripture and answer the following question:

What area of your life currently operates as if it exists for you rather than for Him, and how will you bring it back under His purpose this week?

_____

_____

_____

_____

_____

_____

SHAKE SALT AND SHINE LIGHT

We are called to season the world and to shine light into the darkness around us.

REVIEW, REFLECT, AND RESPOND

As you read Day 57: "Shake Salt and Shine Light" in *Restore: 90 Days of Intentional Living in Faith, Life, and Business*, review, reflect on, and respond to the text by answering the following question.

Evaluate how your presence shifts a room—what must you adjust to radiate light more consistently?

_____

_____

_____

_____

_____

_____

> *"You are the salt of the earth. . . . You are the light of the world."*
>
> —*Matthew 5:13–14 (NIV)*

Consider the scripture and answer the following question:

What environment has grown bland or dim because you've been hesitant to season it or flood it with light?

_____

_____

_____

_____

_____

_____

_____

EXTRAORDINARY LEADERSHIP

Ordinary leaders react to what is.
Extraordinary leaders rise to what could be.

REVIEW, REFLECT, AND RESPOND

As you read Day 58: "Extraordinary Leadership" in *Restore: 90 Days of Intentional Living in Faith, Life, and Business*, review, reflect on, and respond to the text by answering the following question.

What one conversation designed only to ask questions and listen for answers can you schedule this week?

_____

_____

_____

_____

_____

_____

> *"David had served the purpose of God in his own generation."*
>
> —*Acts 13:36 (NIV)*

Consider the scripture and answer the following question:

What is the specific "purpose of God" for you in this current season of leadership?

_____

_____

_____

_____

_____

_____

_____

THE SECRET SAUCE: ASKING GREAT QUESTIONS

*Being prepared with great questions
is the difference-maker.*

REVIEW, REFLECT, AND RESPOND

As you read Day 59: "The Secret Sauce: Asking Great Questions" in *Restore: 90 Days of Intentional Living in Faith, Life, and Business*, review, reflect on, and respond to the text by answering the following question.

What ten thoughtful questions could you keep in a "Question Bank" on your phone to pull from during your next leadership conversation?

_____

_____

_____

_____

_____

_____

> *"Now, O Lord, give your servant a discerning heart."*
>
> —*1 Kings 3:9 (NIV)*

Consider the scripture and answer the following question:

What spiritual discipline could sharpen your discernment so your questions carry greater wisdom?

_____

_____

_____

_____

_____

_____

ROOTED

Are your priorities in order or totally out of whack?

REVIEW, REFLECT, AND RESPOND

As you read Day 60: "Rooted" in *Restore: 90 Days of Intentional Living in Faith, Life, and Business*, review, reflect on, and respond to the text by answering the following question.

What parts of R.O.O.T.S. stood out to you the most, and why?

_____

_____

_____

_____

_____

_____

> *"And the seeds that fell on the good soil represent honest, goodhearted people who hear God's word, cling to it, and patiently produce a huge harvest."*
>
> —Luke 8:15 (NLT)

Consider the scripture and answer the following question:

How does patience factor into producing a "huge harvest," and where have you seen impatience limit growth?

_____

_____

_____

_____

_____

_____

_____

DETERMINE TO DO THE WORK

Prosperity is not automatic. It doesn't just happen because a person loves Jesus.

REVIEW, REFLECT, AND RESPOND

As you read Day 61: "Determine to Do the Work" in *Restore: 90 Days of Intentional Living in Faith, Life, and Business*, review, reflect on, and respond to the text by answering the following question.

What would it look like to "bloom where you are planted" in this specific season of your career or calling?

_____

_____

_____

_____

_____

_____

"Whatever your hand finds to do, do it with all your might."

—Ecclesiastes 9:10 (NIV)

Consider the scripture and answer the following question:

Where might you be holding back effort or excellence, and why?

_____

_____

_____

_____

_____

_____

_____

_____

BREAK FREE FROM A FIXED MINDSET

A faith mindset says, "With God, I can become who I'm called to be."

REVIEW, REFLECT, AND RESPOND

As you read Day 62: "Break Free from a Fixed Mindset" in *Restore: 90 Days of Intentional Living in Faith, Life, and Business*, review, reflect on, and respond to the text by answering the following question.

Which limiting belief has most consistently capped your growth?

_____

_____

_____

_____

_____

_____

"For as he thinks in his heart, so is he."

—*Proverbs 23:7 (KJV)*

Consider the scripture and answer the following question:

What would it look like to transform your inner dialogue about the limiting belief you identified above?

_____

_____

_____

_____

_____

_____

_____

_____

FOCUS: PART 1

*You can't be 100 percent all the time, but you
need to be 100 percent at the right time.*

REVIEW, REFLECT, AND RESPOND

As you read Day 63: "Focus: Part 1" in *Restore: 90 Days of Intentional Living in Faith, Life, and Business*, review, reflect on, and respond to the text by answering the following question.

How do you determine when and where to give your full attention?

_____

_____

_____

_____

_____

_____

> *"Select capable men from all people—men who fear God, trustworthy men who hate dishonest gain— and appoint them as officials over thousands."*
>
> —*Exodus 18:21 (NIV)*

Consider the scripture and answer the following question:

What does this verse teach about the importance of discernment and delegation in leadership, and how does it apply to your life?

_____

_____

_____

_____

_____

_____

FOCUS: PART 2

You can love everyone, but they have to earn your time, and they do that by getting to the top.

REVIEW, REFLECT, AND RESPOND

As you read Day 64: "Focus: Part 2" in *Restore: 90 Days of Intentional Living in Faith, Life, and Business*, review, reflect on, and respond to the text by answering the following question.

Who or what belongs in your top 20 percent of focus this season—and why?

_____

_____

_____

_____

_____

_____

"Be very careful, then, how you live—not as unwise but as wise, making the most of every opportunity."

—*Ephesians 5:15–16 (NIV)*

Consider the scripture and answer the following question:

How does this verse redefine what wisdom looks like in the way you manage your time?

_____

_____

_____

_____

_____

_____

_____

FOCUS: PART 3

When you are at 40 percent, you are not done.

REVIEW, REFLECT, AND RESPOND

As you read Day 65: "Focus: Part 3" in *Restore: 90 Days of Intentional Living in Faith, Life, and Business*, review, reflect on, and respond to the text by answering the following question.

In what area have you been tempted to quit when God might be calling you to persevere?

_____

_____

_____

_____

_____

_____

"He gives strength to the weary and increases the power of the weak."

—Isaiah 40:29 (NIV)

Consider the scripture and answer the following question:

How does acknowledging weakness open the door for divine empowerment? Provide an example from your own life.

_____

_____

_____

_____

_____

_____

FOCUS: PART 4

*You have to be the first to start at
whatever it is that you do.*

REVIEW, REFLECT, AND RESPOND

As you read Day 66: "Focus: Part 4" in *Restore: 90 Days of Intentional Living in Faith, Life, and Business*, review, reflect on, and respond to the text by answering the following question.

What could you start first—taking the initiative before others—to open new doors of impact or growth for you?

_____

_____

_____

_____

_____

_____

"Do nothing out of selfish ambition or vain conceit. Rather, in humility value others above yourself."

—*Philippians 2:3 (NIV)*

Consider the scripture and answer the following question:

How has humility protected you from distraction and pride in pursuing excellence?

_____

_____

_____

_____

_____

_____

YOUR BODY, HIS TEMPLE

Taking care of your body isn't vanity—it's stewardship.

REVIEW, REFLECT, AND RESPOND

As you read Day 67: "Your Body, His Temple" in *Restore: 90 Days of Intentional Living in Faith, Life, and Business*, review, reflect on, and respond to the text by answering the following question.

How does your current health reflect your stewardship of God's resources?

_____

_____

_____

_____

_____

_____

"Do you not know that your bodies are temples of the Holy Spirit? . . . Therefore honor God with your bodies."

—*I Corinthians 6:19–20 (NIV)*

Consider the scripture and answer the following question:

When have you neglected your health in the past, and how did it impact your ability to fulfill the purpose God assigned to you?

_____

_____

_____

_____

_____

_____

_____

OBEDIENCE OVER PERFORMANCE

God doesn't bless performance;
He blesses obedience.

REVIEW, REFLECT, AND RESPOND

As you read Day 68: "Obedience Over Performance" in *Restore: 90 Days of Intentional Living in Faith, Life, and Business*, review, reflect on, and respond to the text by answering the following question.

How does your desire for approval compete with your desire to please God?

_____

_____

_____

_____

_____

_____

> *"Obedience is better than sacrifice."*
>
> —*1 Samuel 15:22 (NLT)*

Consider the scripture and answer the following question:

How does this verse distinguish between doing good things *for* God and doing the right thing *with* God?

_____

_____

_____

_____

_____

_____

_____

_____

BE WHERE YOUR FEET ARE

Presence is the most powerful gift you can give, and it costs you everything and nothing at the same time.

REVIEW, REFLECT, AND RESPOND

As you read Day 69: "Be Where Your Feet Are" in *Restore: 90 Days of Intentional Living in Faith, Life, and Business*, review, reflect on, and respond to the text by answering the following question.

How does your level of presence communicate value to those closest to you?

_____

_____

_____

_____

_____

"This is the day that the Lord has made;
let us rejoice and be glad in it."

—*Psalm 118:24 (NIV)*

Consider the scripture and answer the following question:

What habit could help you notice and celebrate God's presence in ordinary moments?

_____

_____

_____

_____

_____

_____

BEING A SECURE LEADER

Secure leaders are the greatest leaders.

REVIEW, REFLECT, AND RESPOND

As you read Day 70: "Being a Secure Leader" in *Restore: 90 Days of Intentional Living in Faith, Life, and Business*, review, reflect on, and respond to the text by answering the following question.

How does insecurity show up in your leadership decisions, and what emotions or fears usually surface when insecurity drives your choices?

_____

_____

_____

_____

_____

_____

"For we are God's masterpiece. He has created us anew in Christ Jesus, so we can do the good things He planned for us long ago."

—Ephesians 2:10 (NLT)

Consider the scripture and answer the following question:

How can remembering that God planned "good things" for you free you from striving for approval?

_____

_____

_____

_____

_____

_____

_____

BUILDING

When you build something that
honors God, God will honor you.

REVIEW, REFLECT, AND RESPOND

As you read Day 71: "Building" in *Restore: 90 Days of Intentional Living in Faith, Life, and Business*, review, reflect on, and respond to the text by answering the following question.

Where have you seen evidence of God building something through you this year, and how does that differ from times when you tried to build it yourself?

_____

_____

_____

_____

_____

_____

> *"Unless the Lord builds the house, the builders labor in vain."*
>
> —*Psalm 127:1 (author paraphrase)*

Consider the scripture and answer the following question:

How can you tell when your work is being built with God's partnership rather than for your own outcome?

_____

_____

_____

_____

_____

_____

BUILDERS

*Builders build something that the people
can look at and say, "Only God . . ."*

REVIEW, REFLECT, AND RESPOND

As you read Day 72: "Builders" in *Restore: 90 Days of Intentional Living in Faith, Life, and Business*, review, reflect on, and respond to the text by answering the following question.

What distractions most often tempt you to "come down from the wall" before the work is finished?

_____

_____

_____

_____

_____

"Therefore everyone who hears these words of mine and puts them into practice is like a wise man who built his house on the rock."

—*Matthew 7:24 (NIV)*

Consider the scripture and answer the following question:

How have you seen the difference between building wisely and building foolishly play out in your own life?

_____

_____

_____

_____

_____

_____

WHOSE JOB IS IT?

When responsibility is not clearly owned, it's easily abandoned.

REVIEW, REFLECT, AND RESPOND

As you read Day 73: "Whose Job Is It?" in *Restore: 90 Days of Intentional Living in Faith, Life, and Business*, review, reflect on, and respond to the text by answering the following question.

Where have unclear roles or assumptions led to frustration or blame in your work or team, and how could you remedy that?

_____

_____

_____

_____

_____

"Do your best to present yourself to God as one approved, a worker who does not need to be ashamed."

—2 Timothy 2:15 (NIV)

Consider the scripture and answer the following question:

How does your current work ethic reflect the desire to be "approved by God" rather than noticed by others?

_____

_____

_____

_____

_____

_____

THREE LEADERSHIP MINDSETS: PART 1

You have to do less, and you have to let go.

REVIEW, REFLECT, AND RESPOND

As you read Day 74: "Three Leadership Mindsets: Part 1" in *Restore: 90 Days of Intentional Living in Faith, Life, and Business*, review, reflect on, and respond to the text by answering the following question.

How has holding on too tightly slowed your growth or your team's?

_____

_____

_____

_____

_____

_____

> *"You and these people who come to you will only wear yourselves out. The work is too heavy for you; you cannot handle it alone."*
>
> —*Exodus 18:18 (NIV)*

Consider the scripture and answer the following question:

What warning signs of exhaustion—emotional, physical, or spiritual—have you been ignoring that show you're carrying more than God intended?

_____

_____

_____

_____

_____

_____

THREE LEADERSHIP MINDSETS: PART 2

*Sometimes we have problems we can't
solve because we are too close to them.*

REVIEW, REFLECT, AND RESPOND

As you read Day 75: "Three Leadership Mindsets: Part 2" in *Restore: 90 Days of Intentional Living in Faith, Life, and Business*, review, reflect on, and respond to the text by answering the following question.

Which of the three reflection questions in today's reading most challenged your current approach to leadership?

_____

_____

_____

_____

_____

_____

"Do not be anxious about anything, but in every situation, present your requests to God. And the peace of God, which transcends all understanding, will guard your hearts and your minds in Christ Jesus."

—*Philippians 4:6–7 (NIV)*

Consider the scripture and answer the following question:

How does this passage connect higher thinking to inner peace?

_____

_____

_____

_____

_____

_____

THREE LEADERSHIP MINDSETS: PART 3

Your importance isn't determined by what you know but by who you empower.

REVIEW, REFLECT, AND RESPOND

As you read Day 76: "Three Leadership Mindsets: Part 3" in *Restore: 90 Days of Intentional Living in Faith, Life, and Business*, review, reflect on, and respond to the text by answering the following question.

Where in your business or organization could you be strategically absent to create space for others to lead and grow?

_____

_____

_____

_____

_____

"Humble yourselves before the Lord, and he will lift you up."

—*James 4:10 (NIV)*

Consider the scripture and answer the following question:

When was the last time you had to choose humility over being right or being seen, and what did that reveal about your heart?

_____

_____

_____

_____

_____

_____

POSSESSING PASSION

If you have passion, you will pass most people because most people don't have any passion.

REVIEW, REFLECT, AND RESPOND

As you read Day 77: "Possessing Passion" in *Restore: 90 Days of Intentional Living in Faith, Life, and Business*, review, reflect on, and respond to the text by answering the following question.

What stirs the deepest excitement in you right now, and how does it align with God's calling?

_____

_____

_____

_____

_____

_____

"If any of you lacks wisdom, you should ask God, who gives generously to all without finding fault, and it will be given to you."

—James 1:5 (NIV)

Consider the scripture and answer the following question:

What current decision or challenge in your life most requires wisdom rather than emotion or impulse, and how do you plan to navigate that?

_____

_____

_____

_____

_____

DEEP WORK

Shallow work keeps you distracted.

REVIEW, REFLECT, AND RESPOND

As you read Day 78: "Deep Work" in *Restore: 90 Days of Intentional Living in Faith, Life, and Business*, review, reflect on, and respond to the text by answering the following question.

What rhythms or spaces help you do your best, most focused work?

_____

_____

_____

_____

_____

_____

> *"Make it your ambition to lead a quiet life;*
> *you should mind your own business and work*
> *with your hands, just as we told you."*
>
> —*1 Thessalonians 4:11 (author paraphrase)*

Consider the scripture and answer the following question:

What might "minding your own business" look like in a world that glorifies constant noise and comparison?

_____

_____

_____

_____

_____

_____

VISION FIRST, THEN VICTORY

Vision isn't just a leadership tool—
it's a spiritual compass!

REVIEW, REFLECT, AND RESPOND

As you read Day 79: "Vision First, Then Victory" in *Restore: 90 Days of Intentional Living in Faith, Life, and Business*, review, reflect on, and respond to the text by answering the following question.

How clear is the vision guiding your current season of life or work? Review today's reading for guidance and write your vision below.

_____

_____

_____

_____

_____

_____

> *"Commit to the Lord whatever you do, and he will establish your plans."*
>
> —*Proverbs 16:3 (NIV)*

Consider the scripture and answer the following question:

What has resulted from the times you've committed your plans to God versus simply asking Him to bless what you've already decided, and what can you learn from it?

_____

_____

_____

_____

_____

_____

ENTREPRENEURIAL KINGDOM WORK

You're not just an entrepreneur, leader, or businessperson; you're an architect of impact!

REVIEW, REFLECT, AND RESPOND

As you read Day 80: "Entrepreneurial Kingdom Work" in *Restore: 90 Days of Intentional Living in Faith, Life, and Business*, review, reflect on, and respond to the text by answering the following question.

How does seeing your work as kingdom-building rather than business-building change what you're building and why it matters?

_____

_____

_____

_____

_____

_____

> *"Do you see someone skilled in their work? They will serve before kings; they will not serve before officials of low rank."*
>
> —*Proverbs 22:29 (NIV)*

Consider the scripture and answer the following question:

How does this verse challenge the way you view preparation, professionalism, and consistency in your craft?

_____

_____

_____

_____

_____

LESSONS FROM WINSTON CHURCHILL

A real leader always has the capacity for work.

REVIEW, REFLECT, AND RESPOND

As you read Day 81: "Lessons from Winston Churchill" in *Restore: 90 Days of Intentional Living in Faith, Life, and Business*, review, reflect on, and respond to the text by answering the following question.

What specific fear or frustration keeps resurfacing as you press toward your calling, and how are you responding?

_____

_____

_____

_____

_____

_____

> *""But as for you, be strong and do not give up, for your work will be rewarded."*
>
> —*2 Chronicles 15:7 (NIV)*

Consider the scripture and answer the following question:

When have you experienced God's reward come in a form you didn't expect, and what did that teach you about endurance?

_____

_____

_____

_____

_____

_____

_____

ADVICE FOR YOUNGER GENERATIONS

Don't be something you're not.

REVIEW, REFLECT, AND RESPOND

As you read Day 82: "Advice for Younger Generations" in *Restore: 90 Days of Intentional Living in Faith, Life, and Business*, review, reflect on, and respond to the text by answering the following question.

Which of the four life tips have you most intentionally modeled or passed on to someone younger, and what fruit have you seen from it?

_____

_____

_____

_____

_____

_____

> *"We will not hide them from their descendants; we will tell the next generation the praiseworthy deeds of the LORD, his power, and the wonders he has done."*
>
> —*Psalm 78:4 (NIV)*

Consider the scripture and answer the following question:

What stories of God's faithfulness have you personally witnessed that you could share with someone younger this week?

_____

_____

_____

_____

_____

_____

THE MONEY HABIT OF GENEROSITY

We should astound others with our generosity.

REVIEW, REFLECT, AND RESPOND

As you read Day 83: "The Money Habit of Generosity" in *Restore: 90 Days of Intentional Living in Faith, Life, and Business*, review, reflect on, and respond to the text by answering the following question.

How do your current spending and giving habits reflect what you truly value?

_____

_____

_____

_____

_____

_____

"Give, and it will be given to you."

—*Luke 6:38*

Consider the scripture and answer the following question:

What fear or mindset most often keeps you from giving the way this verse describes, and what step of faith could you take this week to give more generously than feels comfortable?

_____

_____

_____

_____

_____

_____

LESSONS FROM THE GREAT JOHN WESLEY

*Keep your thoughts to yourself until you
can sit down and talk with that person.*

REVIEW, REFLECT, AND RESPOND

As you read Day 84: "Lessons from the Great John Wesley" in *Restore: 90 Days of Intentional Living in Faith, Life, and Business*, review, reflect on, and respond to the text by answering the following question.

Which of Wesley's ten leadership lessons most exposes a gap in your own growth?

_____

_____

_____

_____

_____

_____

"The beginning of wisdom is this: Get wisdom. Though it costs all you have, get understanding."

—*Proverbs 4:7 (NIV)*

Consider the scripture and answer the following question:

What specific area of your life or leadership most needs God's wisdom right now?

_____

_____

_____

_____

_____

_____

ALWAYS EXCEED EXPECTATIONS

The quickest way to set yourself apart from others is to exceed expectations!

REVIEW, REFLECT, AND RESPOND

As you read Day 85: "Always Exceed Expectations" in *Restore: 90 Days of Intentional Living in Faith, Life, and Business*, review, reflect on, and respond to the text by answering the following question.

What tangible way could you surprise or bless someone through extraordinary follow-through this week?

_____

_____

_____

_____

_____

"If anyone forces you to go one mile, go with them for two miles."

—*Matthew 5:41*

Consider the scripture and answer the following question:

What relationships or responsibilities in your life currently deserve a "second mile" effort from you?

_____

_____

_____

_____

_____

_____

CONSISTENCY IN LEADERSHIP

Consistency really is a MUST as you build and grow your business.

REVIEW, REFLECT, AND RESPOND

As you read Day 86: "Consistency in Leadership" in *Restore: 90 Days of Intentional Living in Faith, Life, and Business*, review, reflect on, and respond to the text by answering the following question.

Who is watching your example and learning from the steadiness—or lack—of your follow-through?

_____

_____

_____

_____

_____

_____

"Therefore . . . stand firm. Let nothing move you. Always give yourselves fully to the work of the Lord."

—*1 Corinthians 15:58 (NIV)*

Consider the scripture and answer the following question:

How does "giving yourself fully" to God's work challenge your current level of commitment?

_____

_____

_____

_____

_____

_____

HOW TO *REAL* AND NOT WEIRD

God doesn't need you to be perfect—
just present, honest, and available.

REVIEW, REFLECT, AND RESPOND

As you read Day 87: "How to REAL and Not Weird" in *Restore: 90 Days of Intentional Living in Faith, Life, and Business*, review, reflect on, and respond to the text by answering the following question.

Where in your life do you feel pressure to be someone you're not, and what's driving that?

_____

_____

_____

_____

_____

_____

"We refuse to practice cunning . . . [by] the open statement of the truth we would commend ourselves to everyone's conscience in the sight of God."

—*Luke 6:38*

Consider the scripture and answer the following question:

When are you most tempted to perform or hide instead of showing up authentically?

_____

_____

_____

_____

_____

_____

THE THREE MUST-DOs

If your people do not understand the why behind it, they will never rally or buy into the vision.

REVIEW, REFLECT, AND RESPOND

As you read Day 88: "The Three Must-Dos" in *Restore: 90 Days of Intentional Living in Faith, Life, and Business*, review, reflect on, and respond to the text by answering the following question.

When did you last share the "what's in it for them" part with the people you lead?

_____

_____

_____

_____

_____

_____

> *"And the LORD answered me: 'Write the vision; make it plain on tablets, so he may run who reads it.'"*
>
> —*Habakkuk 2:2 (NIV)*

Consider the scripture and answer the following question:

What vision has God placed in your heart that you've never taken time to write down?

_____

_____

_____

_____

_____

_____

_____

THE FOUR PICTURES OF GOD

Remember that every person we encounter in life is either a victim to exploit, a problem to avoid, or a person to be loved.

REVIEW, REFLECT, AND RESPOND

As you read Day 89: "The Four Pictures of God" in *Restore: 90 Days of Intentional Living in Faith, Life, and Business*, review, reflect on, and respond to the text by answering the following question.

Which "picture of God" do you relate to most right now—a locked gate, a garbage can, an endless ladder, or an open door?

_____

_____

_____

_____

_____

_____

"Look! I stand at the door and knock. If you hear my voice and open the door, I will come in, and we will share a meal together as friends."

—Revelation 3:20 (NLT)

Consider the scripture and answer the following question:

What simple prayer of invitation could you pray today to experience deeper friendship with God by opening the door?

_____

_____

_____

_____

_____

BE A GREEN TAG PERSON

We are all called to be tag changers.

REVIEW, REFLECT, AND RESPOND

As you read Day 90: "Be a Green Tag Person" in *Restore: 90 Days of Intentional Living in Faith, Life, and Business*, review, reflect on, and respond to the text by answering the following question.

Who took a risk to believe in you when others didn't, and how can you honor that by doing the same for someone else?

_____

_____

_____

_____

_____

_____

> *"Suppose one of you has a hundred sheep and loses one of them. Doesn't he leave the ninety-nine in the open country and go after the lost sheep until he finds it?"*
>
> —*Luke 15:4 (NIV)*

Consider the scripture and answer the following question:

Who in your life right now represents the "one"—someone overlooked, discouraged, or written off—that God is asking you to pursue?

_____

_____

_____

_____

_____

_____

www.ingramcontent.com/pod-product-compliance
Lightning Source LLC
Chambersburg PA
CBHW080542090426
42734CB00016B/3185